First Science

Build it Strong!

© 1994 Watts Books

First Published in Great Britain
in 1994 by
Watts Books
96 Leonard Street
London
EC2A 4RH

Franklin Watts Australia
14 Mars Road
Lane Cove
NSW 2066

Editorial planning: Serpentine Editorial
Scientific consultant: Dr J.J.M.Rowe

Designed by The R & B Partnership
Illustrator: David Anstey
Photographer: Peter Millard

Additional photographs:
Chris Fairclough Colour Library 8, 18;
G. Ziesler/Bruce Coleman 10;
Leonard Lee Rue/Bruce Coleman 11;
Julian Rowe 13;
Eye Ubiquitous 14;
The Hutchison Library 20;
ZEFA 22;
David Woodfall/NHPA 28.

UK ISBN: 0 7496 1485 4
Dewey Decimal Classification: 531
A CIP catalogue record for this book is
available from the British Library

10 9 8 7 6 5 4 3 2 1

Printed in Malaysia

Build it Strong!

Julian Rowe
and Molly Perham

WATTS BOOKS
London • New York • Sydney

Contents

 SAFETY WARNING
Activities marked with this symbol require the
presence and help of an adult.

Build it!

Build a tower with wooden blocks.
Can you make it firm and strong?

Or will your structure easily fall down?

Brick laying

Have you ever watched a house being built? These bricks are made of clay. They were baked in a very hot oven, or kiln, until they became hard and strong.

Builders use mortar to join bricks together. Mortar is a mixture of sand, cement and water. When it dries, it becomes hard and strong. This girl is using mortar to make a brick wall.

Animal builders

Many birds use clay or mud to build their nests. The mud dries in the sun and becomes hard and firm.

The rufous oven bird in South America makes a round structure of mud, grass and hair.

Beavers use their sharp teeth to cut down trees. They build a large dome-shaped structure of branches and twigs.

The spaces in between the branches are filled with mud. A beaver's home is called a lodge.

Firm foundations

A building needs to stand on firm foundations. If you build on soft sand, the structure sinks down and may fall over.

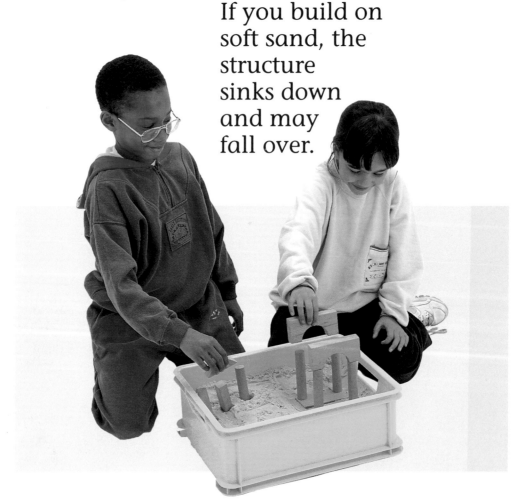

Laying a block underneath spreads out the weight so that the structure stands firm.

Before a house is built, foundations are laid
by pouring concrete into deep trenches.

Roofs

A building needs a strong roof to protect it from the weather. How many different roof shapes can you see in this picture?

Large buildings sometimes have a dome-shaped roof.

The weight of the roof is spread out down the sloping sides of the dome.

Find two large cereal packets, a book and two rulers.

Stand the cereal packets a little way apart to make walls. Open the book in the middle to make a roof.

Now lay the rulers across the cereal packets.

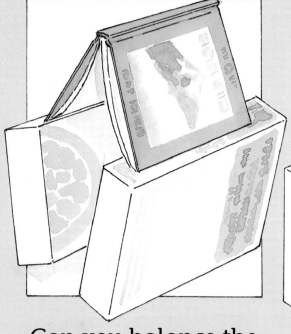

Can you balance the roof on top of the walls? The weight of the roof forces the walls apart.

Can you balance the book now?

Strong shapes

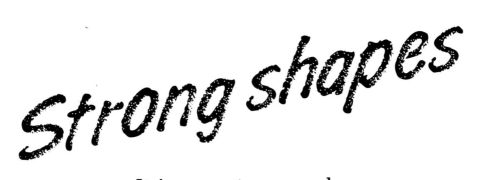

It is easy to squash
a cardboard tube by
squeezing it in the
middle.
It is very difficult to
squash it by pressing
on the ends!

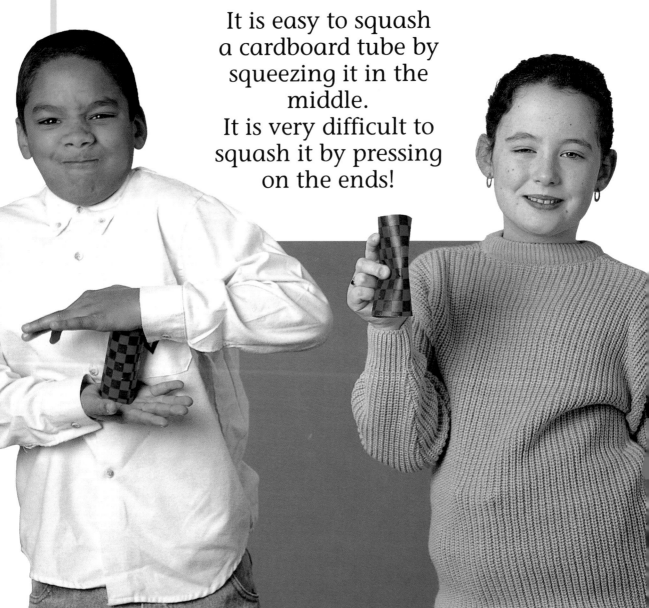

These boxes have strong corners. They can be stacked on top of each other.

A step ladder makes a triangle shape with the floor.

The ladder is strong enough to stand on.

Pylons

Pylons carry heavy
electric cables across
the countryside.
They have to be very
strong so that winds
do not blow them
over.

The lattice structure
is made of thin strips
of steel joined together
in a special pattern.

Can you see any
strong shapes?

Make a pylon

Find some drinking
straws, sticky tape
and some scissors.

Cut short pieces of
sticky tape.
Wrap them round
the ends of the
straws to make a
square shape.

Now start to build your pylon.

What shape makes your tower strong?

19

Carrying weight

The shape of an arch makes it very strong.
The weight above is spread outwards
down the curves.

Strong eggs

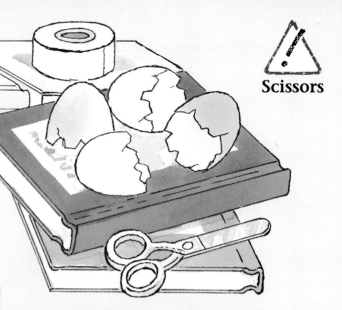

Find four empty eggshells from boiled eggs, masking tape, scissors and some books.

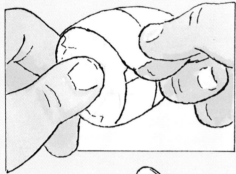

Put some masking tape round the middle of each eggshell.
Carefully cut round the eggshell through the masking tape.

Arrange the eggshells cut side down.

Place a book on top of them.

How many books can you pile up before the shells break?

Bridges

Bridges are made in different shapes and of all kinds of materials.

They can be made from stone, wood, metal or even rope. Suspension bridges are held up by strong steel cables.

How many different shapes of bridge
can you make?

Test how strong your bridge is by placing
weights in the middle.

Travelling light

Some structures are strong but also light. Tents provide a warm and dry place to sleep when you are travelling, and they are light to carry.

Why do they have to be pegged firmly into the ground?

Make a tent

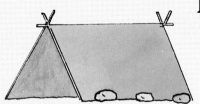

Find a long pole, four short sticks, strong string, an old blanket and some stones.

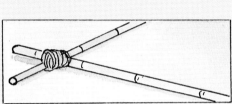

Tie the ends of two sticks together. Do the same with the other two.

Make the frame of the tent by tying the pole across the top. Use string to hold the frame firm.

Put the blanket over the frame and use stones to hold it in place.

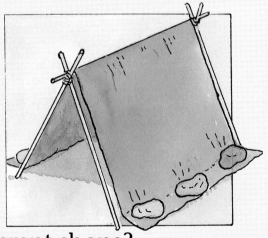

Can you make another tent with a different shape?

Testing materials

Builders need to know the strength of
the materials they use.
One way to do this is to try to break them.
Here paper, plastic and aluminium foil
are being tested.
Which do you think is the strongest?

Wood is glued together to make strong structures in buildings. This boy and girl are testing the strength of their glue.

Acid rain

Poisonous gases from cars and power stations mix with rain and make it acid.

Stone is a strong building material but acid rain makes it weak so that it crumbles away.

See how the figure on this old building has been damaged by acid rain.

How acid rain works

Find a lump of chalk,
some vinegar and
a small plastic bowl.

Put some pieces of
chalk in the bowl.

Pour enough vinegar
over the chalk to
cover it.

What happens to
the chalk?

Vinegar is an acid, like acid rain.
Chalk is like the stone used for building.

Think about... building

Some buildings have a dome-shaped roof. A chain held at each end forms a curve. This is the best shape for a dome.

Coats of varnish protect wood from the weather. Varnish makes the wood waterproof.

Bricks can be laid in many different ways. The way bricks are placed on top of each other is called the 'bond'. These are some different bonds.

These are some of the materials that builders use.

Which of them can you find in your house?